Carving Figural Kaleidoscopes
A New Twist--the "Collide-A-Scope"

Steve Brown

4880 Lower Valley Road, Atglen, PA 19310 USA

Dedication

To everyone that purchases this book, a great big "Thank you."

Contents

Published by Schiffer Publishing Ltd.
4880 Lower Valley Road
Atglen, PA 19310
Phone: (610) 593-1777; Fax: (610) 593-2002
E-mail: Schifferbk@aol.com
Please visit our web site catalog at **www.schifferbooks.com**
We are always looking for people to write books on new and
related subjects. If you have an idea for a book please contact us
at the above address.

This book may be purchased from the publisher.
Include $3.95 for shipping.
Please try your bookstore first.
You may write for a free catalog.

In Europe, Schiffer books are distributed by
Bushwood Books
6 Marksbury Ave.
Kew Gardens
Surrey TW9 4JF England
Phone: 44 (0)20-8392-8585
Fax: 44 (0)20-8392-9876
E-mail: Bushwd@aol.com
Free postage in the UK. Europe: air mail at cost

Copyright © 2003 by Steve Brown
Library of Congress Control Number: 2002113497

Designed by Mark David Bowyer
Type set in Seagull Hv BT/Humanist 521 BT

ISBN: 0-7643-1695-8
Printed in China

Introduction

The name Collide-A-Scope was conceived when I was very young. I grew up in the country, so during the summer I took baths on the back porch. One day while splashing around in our number 4 tub, the tub decided to leave the porch with me aboard. When I "collided" with the ground some 4 1/2 feet later, all I remember was seeing stars and all these beautiful colors. From this small occurrence, some forty years later, the "Collide-A-Scope" was born. With the step-by-step instructions, along with the Collide-A-Scope kits, you are going to create a very unique carving.

First, we will take a look at the roughout and then get familiar with the components of the Collide-A-Scope. A section on painting the Wizard and, for those who wish to cut their own blanks patterns and measurements are included. The full color gallery will help put your imagination in gear to create new and wonderful "Collide-A-Scopes."

Lets get going!

General Notes

Tools: The tools listed were used on the project and gallery pieces. Palm chisels used 1/16 inch, 1/8 inch; 1/4 inch v tools, 1/8 inch; 1/4 inch veiners; 3/16 inch #9 gouge; 1/2 inch #3 gouge; 1/2 inch #9; and a fixed blade carving knife. Other supplies needed: silicone glue, acrylic paint, lacquer, 1 inch dowel rod or broom handle, and instant glue.

Wood: All of the Collide-A-Scopes were carved from the Collide-A-Scope kit available from Wood Carving Suppliers nation wide or from the author, Steve Brown, 1805 Forest Acres Loop, Madisonville, KY 42431.

Carving Without a Kit: For those carvers who choose not to purchase a kit, here are steps and dimensions to make the Wizard Collide-A-Scope. Using the Wizard pattern provided, transfer the front and side patterns onto a 4" x 4" x 13" piece of basswood. Bandsaw around both views. Remove the hat from the blank at this time using the bandsaw. Cut along the hat brim line.

At the bottom of the blank, locate the center and drill a 1 1/2-inch hole, 1 1/2 inches deep. Next drill a 1 1/8-inch hole approximately 8 inches deep. The depth of this hole can vary, just make sure to leave at least 1-inch or more between the hat and the top of the 1 1/8-inch hole. Now drill a 3/8-inch hole through the rest of the blank. This would be the area between the 1 1/8-inch hole and the hat. Next drill a 3/8-inch hole in the bottom of the hat 1/2-inch deep. Glue a 1 1/2-inch long 3/8-inch dowel in the cap.

Cut a 1/2-inch hole in the center of a 3 x 3-inch piece of 1/32-inch thick cardboard. The cardboard from the back of a writing tablet works great. Glue the cardboard to the area where the hat was cut from the blank. Make sure to center the cardboard hole over the 3/8-inch hole in the blank. Now glue the hat to the cardboard. Be careful not to get any glue on the dowel. After the glue has dried, start doing the fun part ... carving!

Let's go.

Wizard Collide-A-Scope
Roughout and Collide-A-Scope Components

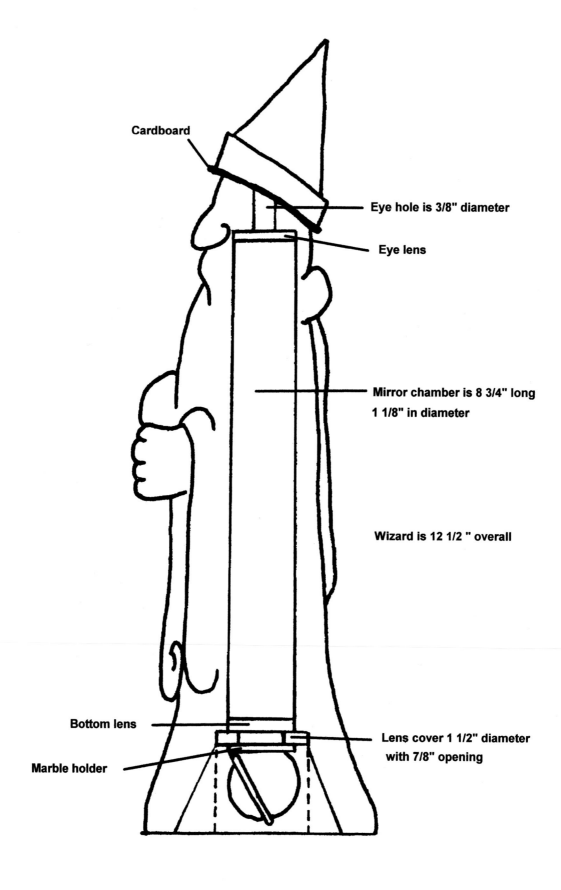

Cardboard

Eye hole is 3/8" diameter

Eye lens

Mirror chamber is 8 3/4" long
1 1/8" in diameter

Wizard is 12 1/2 " overall

Bottom lens

Marble holder

Lens cover 1 1/2" diameter
with 7/8" opening

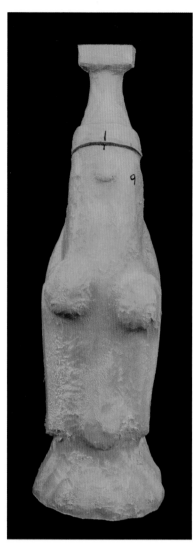

During the manufacturing of the kits, the hat is cut from the body, there is a centerline drawn and a number is written on the body and hat. This is done to keep the corresponding hat with the body as it is being drilled.

The dark line at the bottom of the hat is cardboard. During manufacturing, the cardboard is glued onto the hat and body after all drilling has been completed.

The hat is glued back onto the body during manufacturing. This is done so all chisel and knife cuts will match when carving is completed.

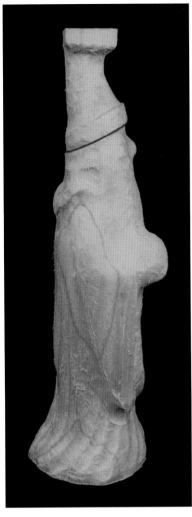

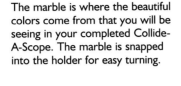

The marble is where the beautiful colors come from that you will be seeing in your completed Collide-A-Scope. The marble is snapped into the holder for easy turning.

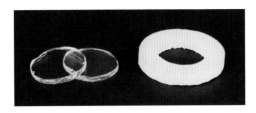

One glass lens will be placed inside the head area and the other lens is installed at the bottom of the robe area. The wood lens cover will be glued over the bottom lens. The marble holder will be glued to the wood lens cover.

From right to left: A small piece of wood will be used for the Wizard's staff. The three mirrors are used to deliver the beautiful colors to your eyes. There are three long and two short pieces of foil tape. The tape is used to hold the mirrors together.

After carving has been completed the removal of the hat from the body will be discussed.

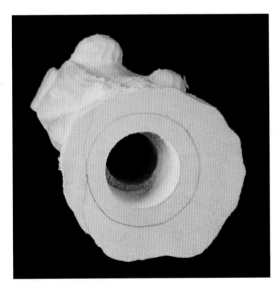

Bottom view of the roughout showing the opening where the components will be placed.

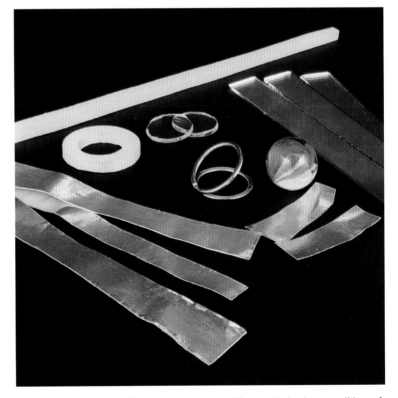

Another view of all the Wizard's components. There will also be a small bag of Styrofoam included in the kit to hold mirrors in the mirror chamber. Please remember, when the carving process begins, there is a hole in the roughout. Don't carve to deep. Familiarize yourself with the component pattern on page four.

Carving the Roughout

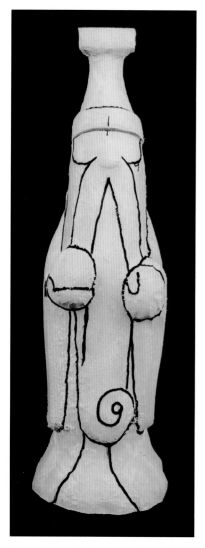

Front view of roughout with detail lines drawn on.

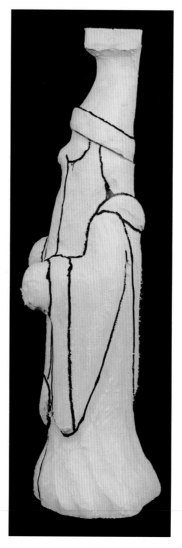

Left side view with detail lines drawn on.

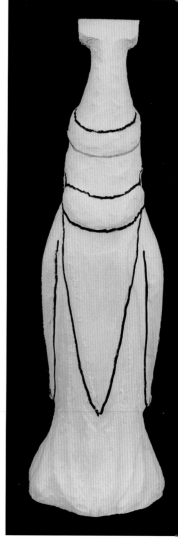

Back view with detail lines drawn on. There will be other detail lines draw on during the carving process.

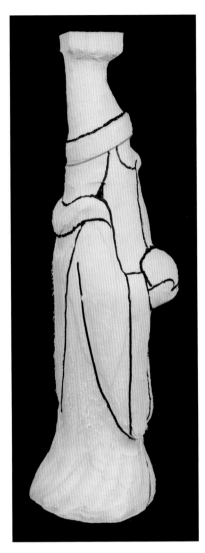

Right side with detail lines drawn on.

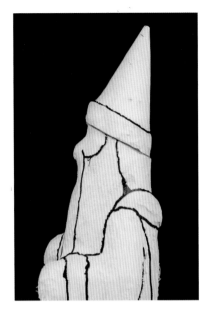

Left view of how the hat is taking shape. Continue to remove wood with your knife until the hat looks like a cone.

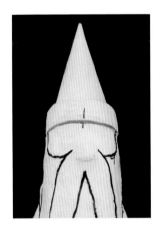

Put a v cut around the brim of the hat brim using a 1/4 inch v tool.

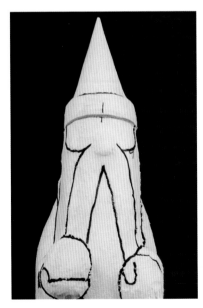

With the carving knife, start shaping the hat by removing the large knob of wood at the top of roughout.

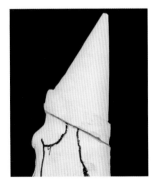

After the v cut around brim is finished, smooth the v cut into the cone shape.

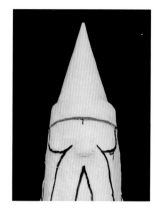

A carving knife was used to remove the rough areas from the brim.

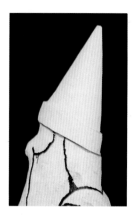

Continue cleaning the brim area with your knife until all roughness has been smoothed.

Make a similar v cut under the brim at the cardboard location.

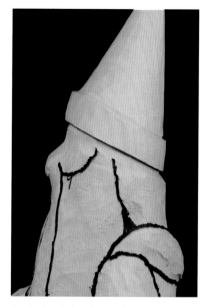

Angle the 1/4 inch v tool so more wood is removed toward the face and hair.

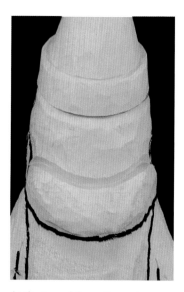

At the top of the collar make a cut. The 1/4 inch v tool will not be angled on this cut.

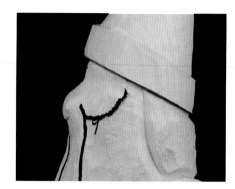

On the left side, where the hair and beard meet, make a v cut with the 1/4 inch v tool. Angle the cut more toward the beard.

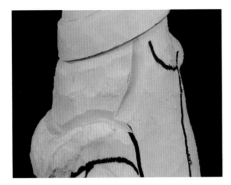

Make the same cut on the right side. Make sure the 1/4 inch v tool is angled toward the beard.

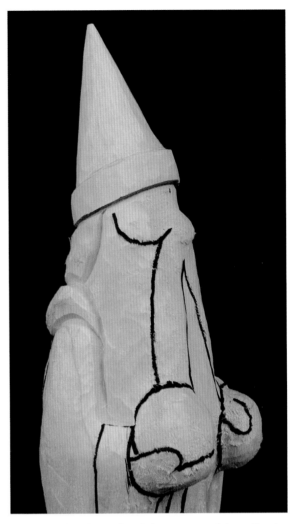

With the 1/4 inch v tool angled more toward the cuff and arm, make this v cut.

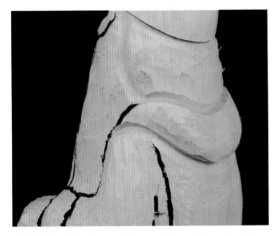

Angle the 1/4 inch v tool toward the robe and make the v cut under the collar and continue the cut over the shoulder.

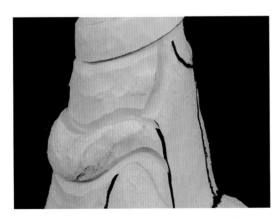

View of the same cut, only over the right shoulder.

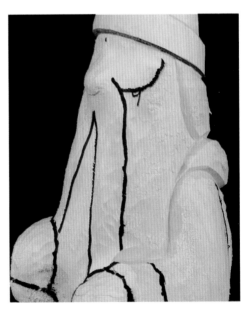

The left cuff and arm gets the same cut. After making these cuts, angle the 1/4 inch v tool toward the beard and make another v cut.

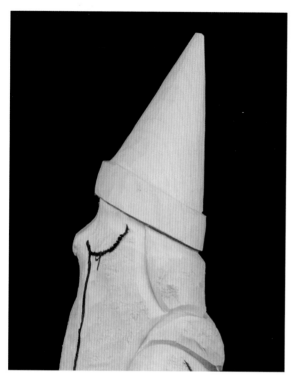

Place the carving knife at the tip of the nose and make a flat sweeping cut up to the brim of the hat. This cut sets the top of the nose and the forehead.

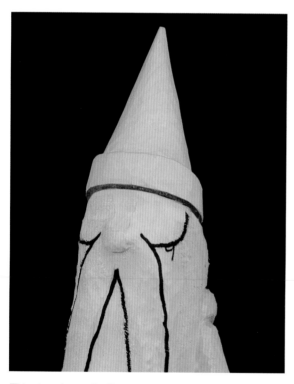

This view shows the flat sweeping cut made with the knife.

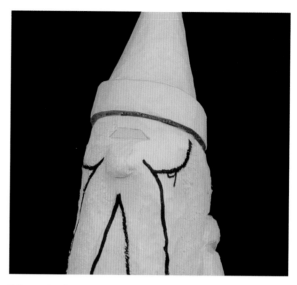

Where the flat sweeping cut turns up, make a v cut with the knife. The v cut will be around 1/2 inch long.

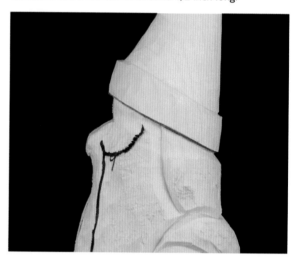

Side view of the v cut made with the knife. This cut separates the nose from the forehead.

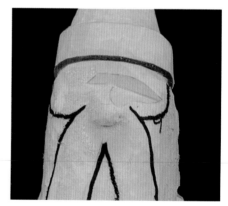

Place the carving knife against the upper angle of the v cut that was just made. Push down on the knife, putting more pressure at the heel of the knife. This makes a stop cut that angles from the center of the nose down toward the temple area. Set the knife at the end of the nose and angled down slightly. Push the knife up toward the stop cut. The cut should look similar to the one pictured.

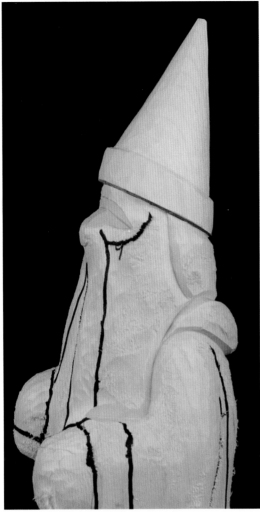

A different view of the angles just cut.

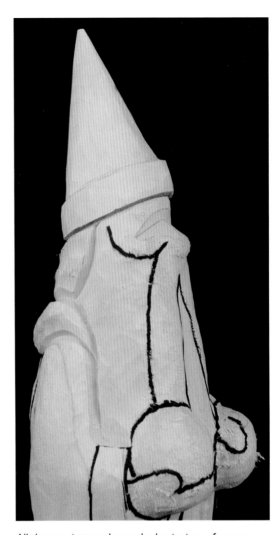

All the cuts just made are the beginnings of a very unique carving. Keep it up!

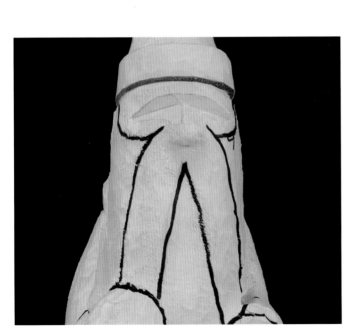

Repeat the last steps to cut the opposite side.

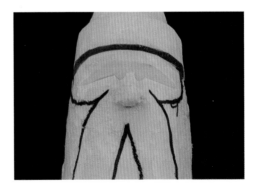

To form the bridge of the nose, use a 1/8 inch veiner to make a cut starting just behind where the nostril will be located. Push the veiner all the way up to where the angle cut was made with the knife in the last step. Repeat this veiner cut for opposite side of the nose. These two veiner cuts will form the bridge of the nose.

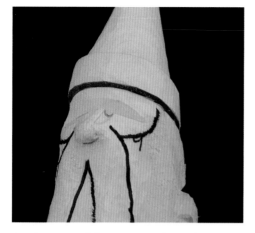

Another view of the veiner cut that makes the bridge of the nose. Various size veiners and gouges can be used on these cuts to create a steep or shallow bridge.

Both edges from the veiner cuts have been removed. The planes where the eyes will be carved have also been established.

The knife was used to remove the edge of wood that was left when the veiner cut was made. Make the cut from where the veiner started and continue to the outside point at the temple area. This view shows the before and after the knife cut.

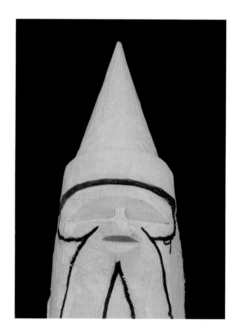

Make this next v cut with the knife. This cut will establish the lower portion of nose. Leave a small area of wood for the tip of the nose; now set the knife at a very slight angle and push down. Finish this v cut by placing the knife about 3/16 inch below the last cut and push up.

View of the knife cut and how it cleans that area up.

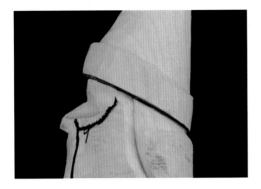

The slight downward angle under the nose can be seen here.

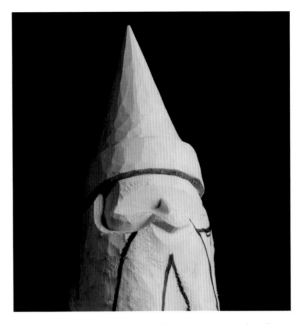

The line drawn from the nostril flare down around and up to the hat creates the cheek, temple, and the upper edge of the beard. Using the 1/4 inch v tool, start the cut at mid-cheek and cut up to the hat. Now make the cut from mid-cheek up to the nostril flare. Lean the v tool so it will round the cheek area, reduce the temple width, and start the flare of the nose.

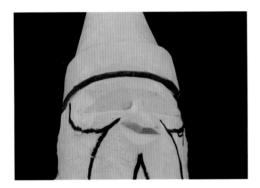

From the center of the nose tip, cut an area where the nostrils will be placed. Hold the knife at the tip of the nose and angle the knife tip up toward the temple. Push the knife down, making the cut. Complete the v cut by pushing the knife up, removing the wood.

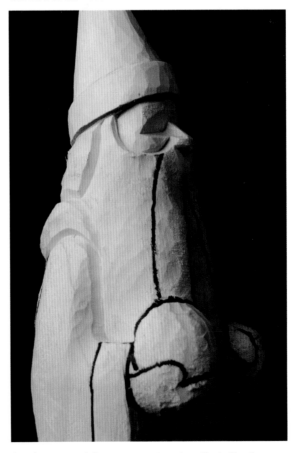

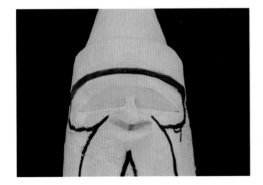

Using the same cuts, carve the opposite side of nose.

Another view of the same cuts just described. Continue using the 1/4 inch v tool and cut the opposite side.

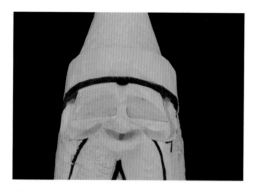

The forehead area has been divided to create the brows. Use the 3/16 #9 gouge and push the gouge from the end of the bridge to the hat brim.

Angle view of how the eyebrow mound is shaping up.

Carve a mound in the area where the eye brows will be with the 1/4 inch v tool.

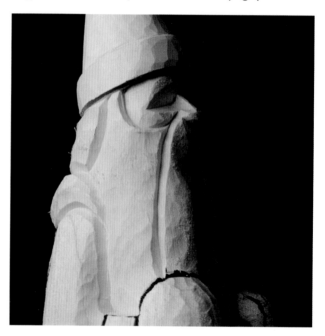

With the 1/4 inch v tool, separate the mustache from the beard. Push the v tool from the crystal ball up to back of the nose flare.

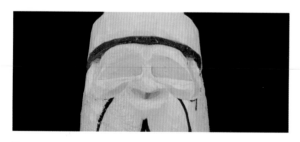

The opposite eyebrow mound has been carved.

The opposite mustache line is cut with the 1/4 inch v tool

Make a stop cut along the nose flare. Then make a stop cut down the mustache cut about 1/4 inch long. There have been two stop cuts made, forming a pie shape. With the knife, cut the piece of pie away. As you are cutting, turn the knife so it shapes the mustache, rounding that area slightly.

Just by making these few simple cuts, the nose goes from setting out on the face or looking flat to a nose set into the face.

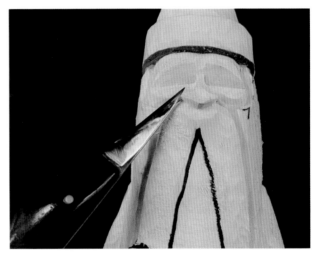

To reduce the thickness of the cheek and flat area under the eye, place the knife at the back of the nose flare with the cutting edge toward the eye. Make this cut with one sweeping motion from the back of the nostril toward the temple area.

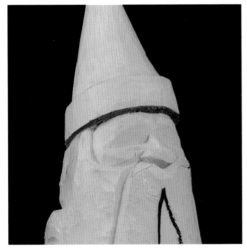

The knife has been removed from the picture and the area just described has been penciled in so it may be seen better.

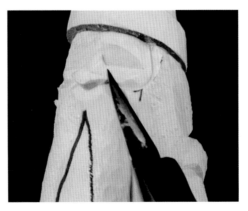

Repeat the last step for the opposite cheek area.

Draw in the shape of the eyes.

Draw a center line through the eyes.

Always cut the eyelids from center to left to minimize chipping (a good sharp v tool will also help). With the 1/16 inch v tool, make the cut on half of the upper portion of the lid.

To carve the other half of the upper lid, hold the roughout upside down. Now the cuts will be from center to left.

Still using the 1/16 inch v tool, make the cut on half of the lower portion of the lid.

Turn the roughout upside down and complete the eyelid cut.

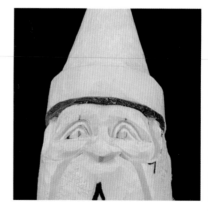

Make two stop cuts in one corner of the eyeball. These cuts are made with the knifepoint. Again, the stop cuts have formed the shape of a piece of pie again. Using the tip of the knife, reach in and remove the piece. Do not go straight in to remove the pie shape. Lean the knife toward the nose. This will give it more of a round appearance.

Continue to make stop cuts in the other corners and removing the pie shaped pieces.

Reduce the width of the nose by using the knife. If the nose does not look too wide, go to the next step.

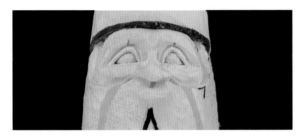

Remove the pencil marks from the eyeball with the tip of the knife. Just removing the pencil mark makes the eyeball look round.

Round up the cheek area with your knife. Do this to the opposite cheek.

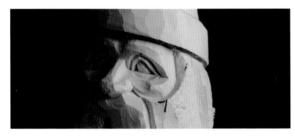

Look closely under the eyeball. There has been a bag carved. With the 1/16 inch v tool, make this cut. It is best to go from right to left on this v cut. Make this same cut under the other eye.

Turn either the 1/8 inch veiner or the 3/16 inch gouge upside down. Then cut one of the nostrils carefully. Do not push straight in because it may pop the nose off of the carving.

Both nostrils have been cut.

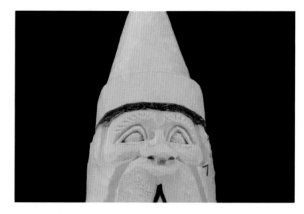

Using the 1/16 inch v tool, cut in the hair on the brows. It's coming alive!

Using the knife, remove the wood just above where the eyebrow will be located. This will create a mound for the brow. Do this on both sides.

While the 1/16 inch v tool is in hand, make a few light cuts at the temple area to form crows foot wrinkles. Also make a few v cuts under the eye to form more wrinkles.

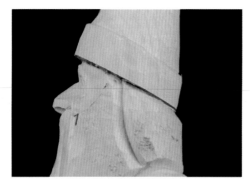

As this side view shows, there was not but just a small amount of wood removed between the top of the brow and hat brim.

Wrinkles have been cut under the left eye.

Remove the edge from the beard. Smooth the beard down to the cheek area.

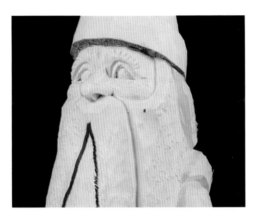

The left side of beard has been smoothed down to the cheek.

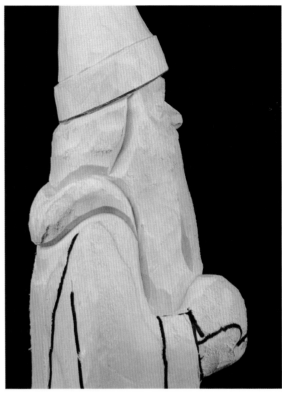

Cut around the crystal ball with the 1/4 inch v tool. Use both flats of the v tool to widen the cut.

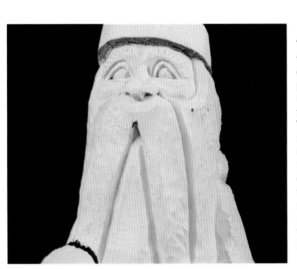

The 1/4 inch v tool was used to cut the lower part of the mustache up to the mouth. Where the mustache meets under the nose, make two stop cuts. The cuts will form an upside down v. Cut this pie shape out with the knife. Now he can eat!

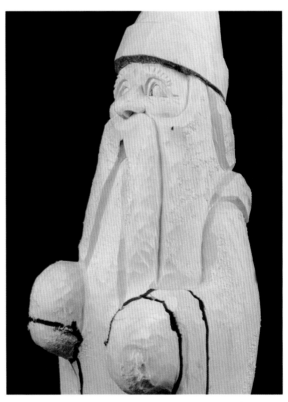

The v cut on the other side of the crystal ball.

The thumb has been cut around with the 1/4 inch v tool. Don't you just love this tool?

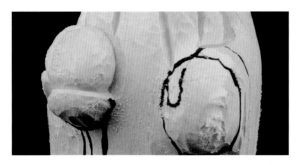

The outline of the right hand where the finger tips will be has been cut with the 1/4 inch v tool.

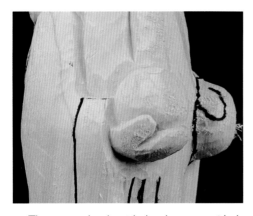

The area under the right hand was cut with the 1/4 inch v tool.

Remove some of the bulk from top of the left hand. Cut around the thumb and the hand with the 1/4 inch v tool.

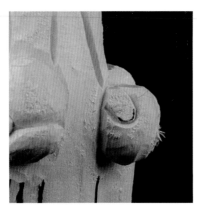

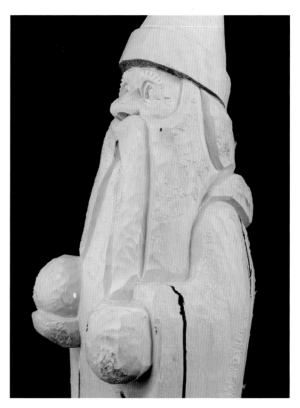

View of the cut made to the back of the left hand.

The 1/4 inch v cut made to the cuff where it lays against the robe.

The right sleeve and cuff were cut with the v tool. Again, only make the sleeve cut up to the armpit.

Make a v cut to form the width of the cuff. Now make a deep v cut to form the sleeve. Do not make the sleeve cut up to the shoulder, only to the armpit area.

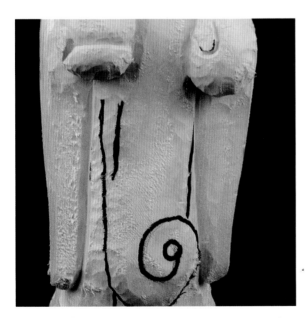

The front of the right cuff has been cut with guess what?

Outline the beard and around the curl of the beard with the 1/4 inch v tool. Also make a v cut where the mustache continues under the right hand.

23

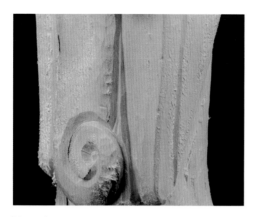

View showing cuts around the curl of the beard.

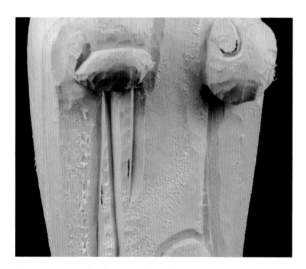

Separate the robe from the skirt by making a v cut.

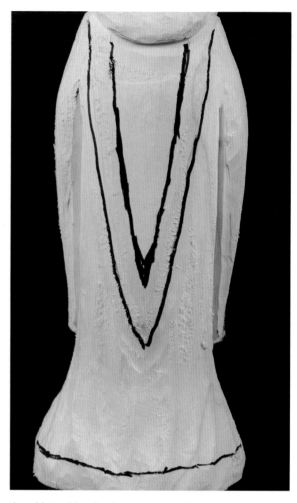

An additional line has been drawn to form the border of the cape.

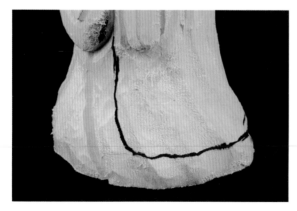

A line has been drawn in for the border of the robe.

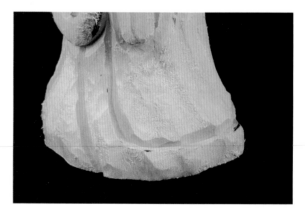

Make deep v cuts around the border of the robe. Continue the cut around to the opposite side.

The border of cape has been laid in with the v tool. That will be it for the 1/4 inch v tool for awhile.

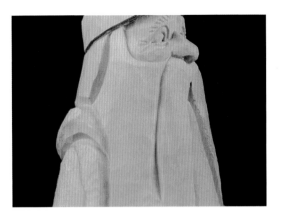

Remove the rough areas from the beard and mustache with the knife.

Now the knife takes over. Smooth out the hair area of the head.

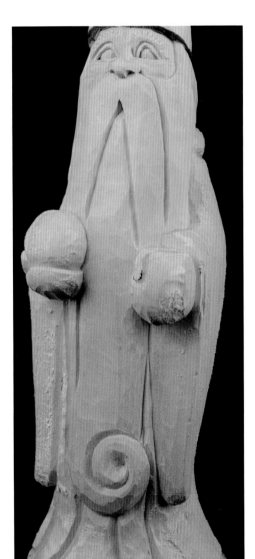

The rest of the beard has been smoothed. Deepen the area where the curl ends with the tip of the knife.

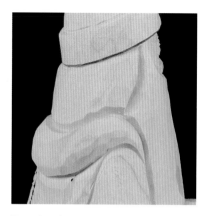

Round and smooth the collar.

The border of the cuff has been smoothed. At this time, clean up the right cuff.

The crystal ball has been rounded and smoothed with the knife.

Smooth both sleeves. Remove all roughness. This is a good view of the crystal ball and how it looks against the beard.

The right hand is taking shape after it is smoothed.

View of how the right hand looks against the beard.

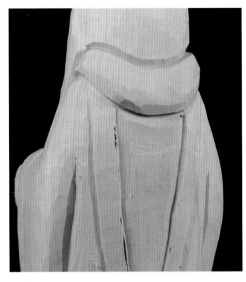

Smooth the border of the cape with the knife.

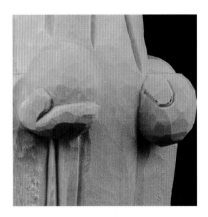

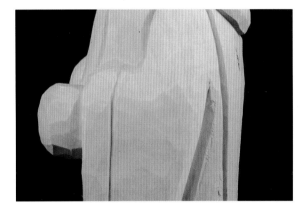

The back of the left hand has been smoothed.

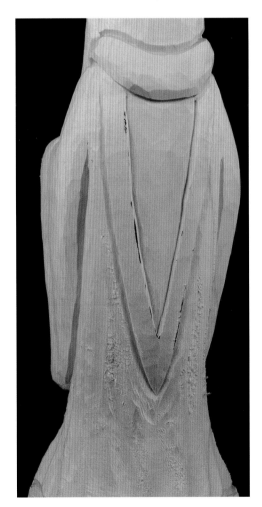

The cape area has been smoothed.

Draw the area inside the cuff as pictured.

The left border of the robe under the curl of the beard has been shaped with the knife.

Using the 1/4 inch v tool, make deep, deep cuts to the inside area of the cuffs. Finish these cuts by using the knife to make the v cuts deeper and sharper. Also, clean the front of the cuffs with the knife.

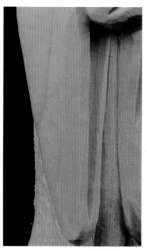

The right border of the robe between the cuff and beard has been cleaned of roughness.

The knife and 1/2 inch #9 gouge were used to cut a few large wrinkles in the skirt. Draw in a shoe under the bottom wrinkle.

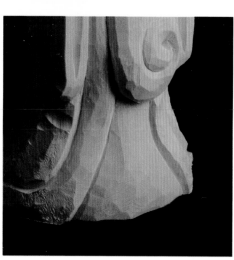

To form the front of the shoe, the 1/4 inch v tool was used.

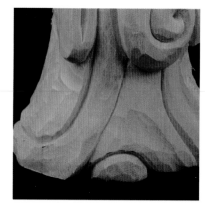

The skirt under the curl of the beard has been smoothed.

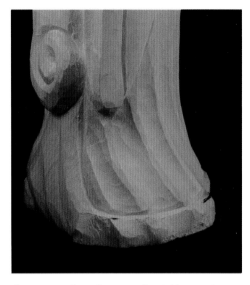

Continue making the gouged wrinkles coming around the front and up to the cuff. Do this on the right side in the same manner.

The roughout has ridges on the robe where the wrinkles are to be placed. With the knife, cut the ridges down. The robe has also been smoothed just behind left sleeve. Repeat this procedure on the right side.

Between the ridges just removed, push the 1/2 inch #9 gouge up to the area on the robe. Do not go as deep as you approach the smooth area of the robe. Do this on the right side, also.

Nice view of the gouged wrinkles on the robe's right side.

Smooth out the bottom border all the way around with the knife.

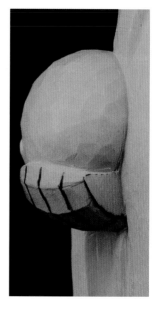

Wood has been removed from the side of the little finger and index finger.

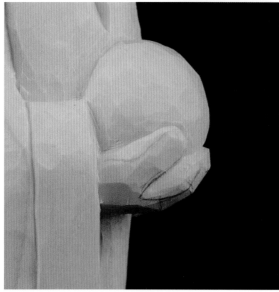

Including the wrist, the hand has four planes. The planes get shorter as they progress to the tips. Make these planes with the knife. The thumb has three planes.

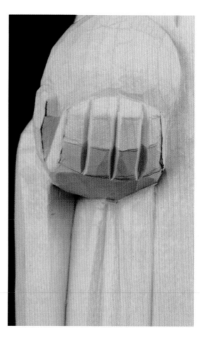

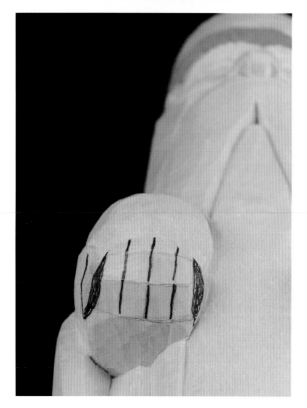

Draw in the fingers. The black areas on the side of the index and little finger represent excess wood that will be removed.

Now, with the 1/8 inch v tool, cut between each finger.

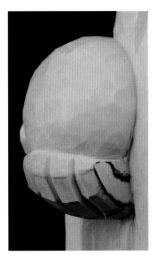

Draw the side of the little finger.

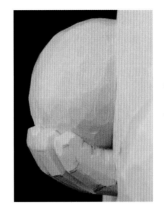

The small wrinkles where the little finger bends were made with the knife tip.

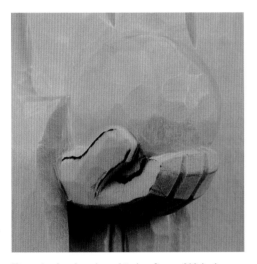

Draw in the thumb and index finger. With the 1/8 inch v tool, cut in the shape of the thumb. Make sure to keep the shape of the crystal ball.

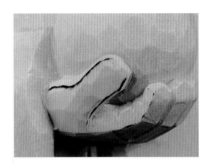

The wrinkles where the index finger bends were made with the knife tip.

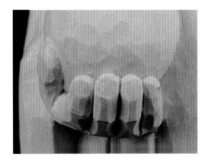

Round up each finger and thumb with the knife. Flatten an area at the end of each finger and thumb.

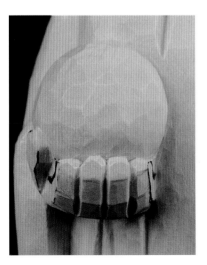

The knife was used to round up the finger tips.

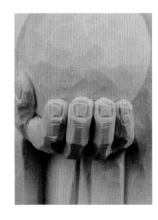

In the flat areas, carve in the fingernails with the 1/16 inch v tool. With the same v tool, cut in small straight bend marks on each joint.

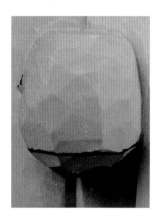

Draw a line indicating the bottom of the left hand.

Draw in the width of the fingers.

Using the knife and 1/4 inch v tool, remove the wood below the line on the left hand.

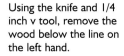

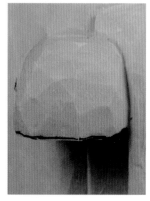

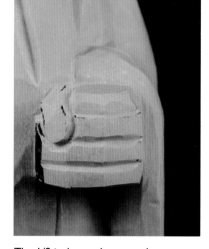

The 1/8 inch v tool was used to separate the fingers.

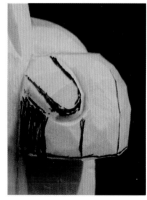

Draw in the four planes of the hand. Darken in the wood that's remaining at the fingertips. This area will be removed.

With the knife, remove the black area at the finger tips

Cut the planes of the left hand with the knife. Remember each plane gets shorter in length as it progresses to the fingertip.

Round the fingers and thumb with the knife. Put a flat area at the end of fingers for the fingernails. Round the fingertips with the knife.

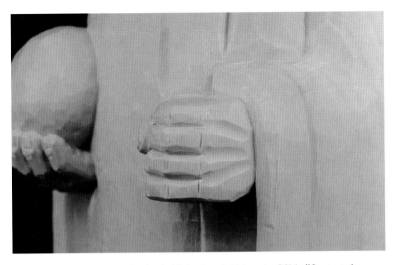

Put three gouge cuts on the back of the hand. Using the 3/16 #9, start the cuts where the v tool cuts stopped. This would be the knuckle area.

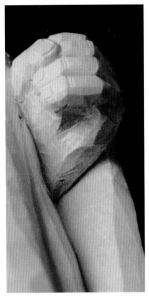

Give shape to the forehand and little finger with the knife and 1/8 inch veiner. Do not carve all the way through the hand.

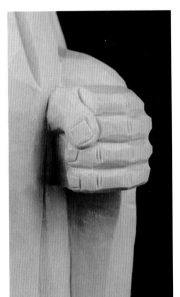

Carve in the fingernails and the straight cuts at each joint where the fingers bend.

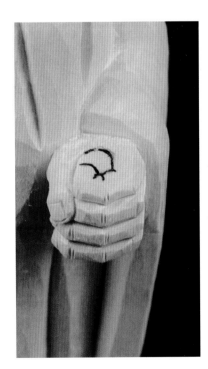

Draw the top of the index finger and hand. Since the hand will be holding a staff, the finger would not touch the palm of the hand.

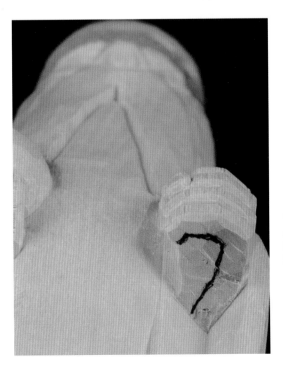

The bottom shape of the hand has been drawn.

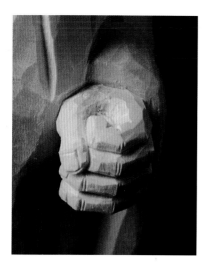

The 1/16 inch v tool and 1/8 inch veiner was used to form the finger and the area around the thumb.

By moving the v tool in different directions, it creates this great looking fur. Just remember, push and pick.

Now to making fur. Using the 1/16 inch v tool, push it in and pick it out. Turn the v tool upside down, sideways; make the fur go in different directions.

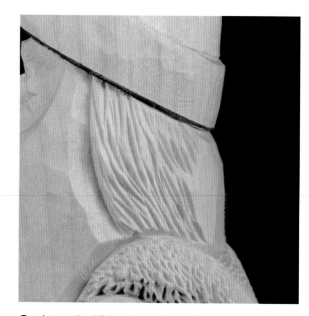

Combining the 1/16 inch v tool and 1/8 inch v tool, start carving in the hair. Stagger the cuts. Don't make one continuous v cut from bottom to top.

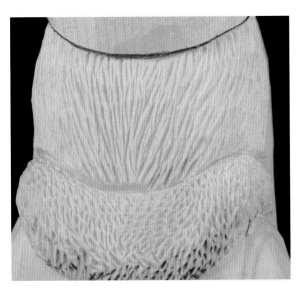

Continue carving the hair with the v tools.

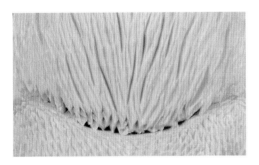

Turn the 1/16 inch v tool upside down, then push and pick at the end of the hair. Where the hair hits the collar, use the knife tip to make random cuts. This will help separate hair from the robe's collar.

Using the same two v tools, start cutting the hair for the beard. Don't let the v tools mark the cheek.

After carving the right side of the beard down to the sleeve, start cutting in the mustache with the v tools. Continue the v cuts on the left mustache and beard.

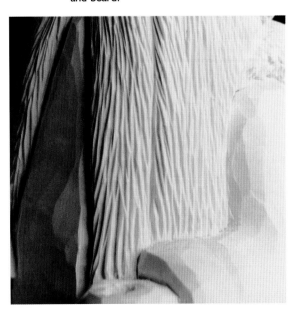

Both sides of the mustache and beard have been carved down to each sleeve.

Where the beard meets the cheek, make small random v cuts. This separates strands of hair so the cheek can be seen and it breaks that one solid line of beard.

Carve the bottom lip by using the 1/8 inch veiner. Push the veiner in both directions, and then clean the edge where it meets the beard with the knife.

Turn the 1/16 v tool upside down, then push and pick the ends of the beard where it meets the collar and sleeve. Use the tip of the knife and make narrow but deep v cuts randomly in the beard.

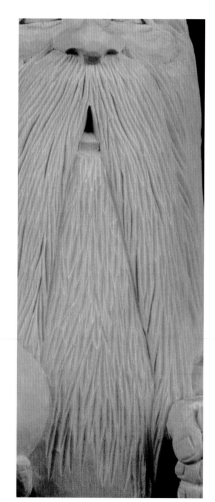

The beard under the lip was carved with the same v tools. Continue staggering the cuts.

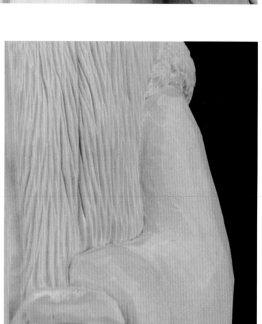

The left side of the beard down to the sleeve has been carved. Notice the random narrow v cuts made with the knife.

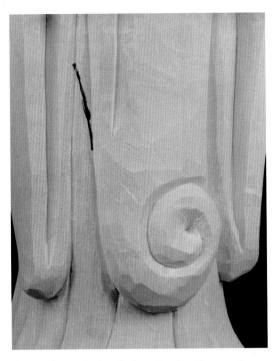

Draw a line widening the beard so it will run under the right cuff. The lower part of the beard did not flow with the upper part, which is why this was done.

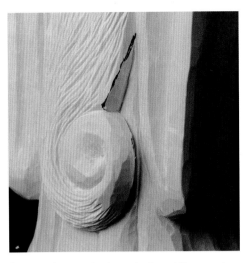

Remove the wood where the beard flows under the left cuff and the curl of the beard. Use the knife and 1/8 inch v tool.

Remove the wood from this area with the knife.

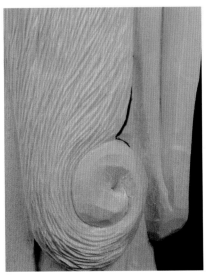

Continue carving the lower portion of the beard with the v tools. Draw the line where the beard will flow under the left cuff.

Finish carving the beard and curl with the v tools. The knife was used to make narrow deep v cuts.

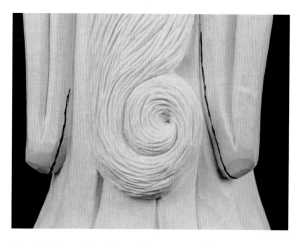

Draw in lines where the cuff lays against the robe. Undercuts will be made here.

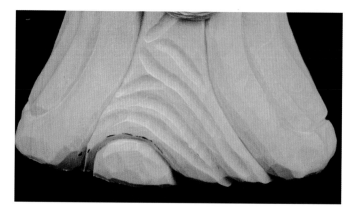

The 1/4 inch veiner was used to start the wrinkles in the skirt. Continue with the veiner down past the base of the roughout, creating a wrinkle that is turned under.

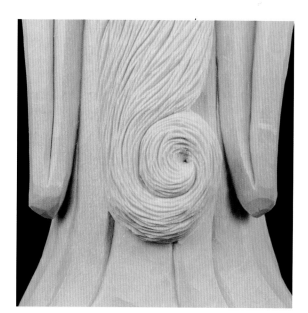

The knife was used to undercut the bottom of the cuff.

Round the edges made by the 1/4 inch veiner with the knife.

Draw in a line for the shoe sole.

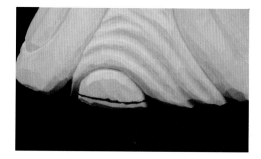

Draw in some lines for wrinkles on the skirt.

The shoe sole was cut using the 1/8 inch v tool. The edges were rounded with the knife.

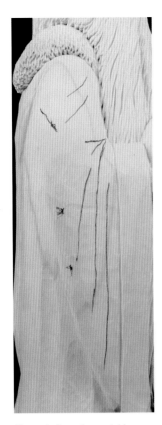

Draw in lines for wrinkles on both the sleeves.

Wrinkles running down the sleeve were made with the 1/4 inch veiner.

View of the left sleeve wrinkles. Smooth all the edges made with the gouge and veiner. This should also be done on the right sleeve wrinkles.

The wrinkles on the shoulder were made with the 1/2 inch #9 gouge. Wrinkles at the bend of the elbow were made with the 1/8 inch v tool. Edges of cuts were smoothed with the knife. Make all of these cuts on the left arm as well.

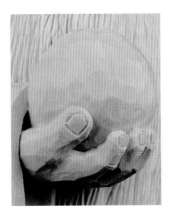

This small detail helps to round up the crystal ball. Use the knife to make a small v cut behind the ball into the cuff.

The knife tip was used to make a narrow v cut around the wrist of the left hand.

Holding the carving, twist the hat back and forth until it lets go. If, after twisting a couple times, the hat does not come off, just scribe around the cardboard once more.

Now on to removing the hat. Using the knife tip, scribe all the way around the cardboard. This will probably have to be done at least three times. Make sure the wood on the hat and hair are not being cut.

The wizard without his hat.

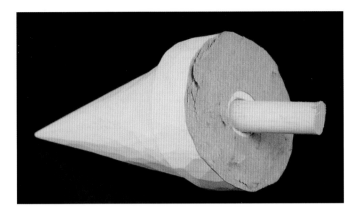

The dowel rod is what keeps the hat from falling off.

Trim excess wood from the cover up to the reference line. Insert the lens cover into the opening. When the cover stops, draw a line around the cover onto the inside opening. Notice in the photo that the line has already been drawn on the bottom of the carving.

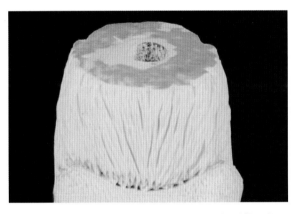

To remove the cardboard, use the knife and the 1/2 inch #3. Leaving traces of the glue behind will be okay; just don't remove any wood.

Using the knife, taper the opening from the line drawn on the bottom to the line that was just drawn on the inside.

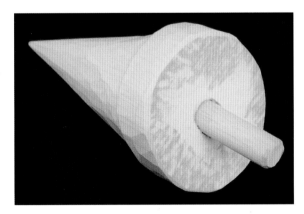

Use the same method to remove the cardboard from the hat.

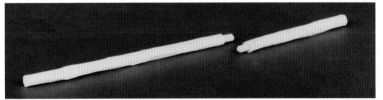

Set the carving on a flat surface, measure the length from the surface to the bottom of the left hand, then add 1/2 inch. Cut the wood provided in the kit for the staff accordingly. This piece of wood for the staff measures 1/4 inch square by 10 inches long overall. Now cut a small peg in the ends that will go into the hand. Round up the outside of the wood to form the staff.

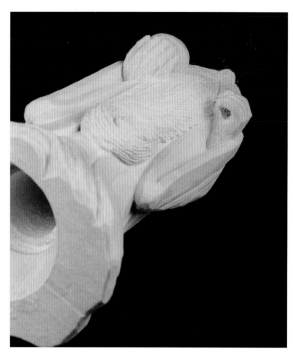

Wrap sandpaper around a piece of broom handle or a 1 inch dowel rod long enough to reach the length of the mirror chamber and then sand the chamber. It does not have to be completely smooth. Knock off the fuzzies.

In the left hand, remove enough wood so the pegs in the staff will fit. The lower part of the staff should fit so it will lay against the robe.

The staff has been rounded and fit to the hand. A good way to get a perfect length on the lower part of the staff is to set the carving at the edge of a flat surface, move the carving until the staff hits the flat surface. Draw a mark where the staff hits the edge. Then cut the excess off with the knife. Do not glue the staff yet. Just remove it and lay the staff aside.

The inside of the mirror chamber must be sealed to keep small wood particles from coming loose. Hold a finger over the eyehole while pouring sealer into the chamber. Make sure the entire chamber is coated. Lacquer was used on the wizard for the fast drying time. After the sealer has been poured in, hold the carving over the container and remove your finger. Let the excess drip from the eyehole. Let dry.

This view shows residue from the lacquer. The tapered area at the base does not need to be sealed but if it is, it will not harm the carving.

Painting the Wizard

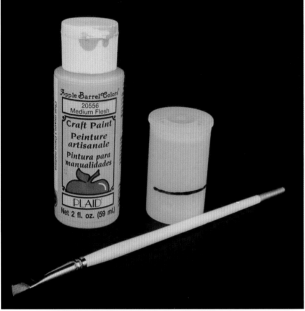

Acrylic paint was used on all the carvings in this book. No certain brand, just whatever the local department store handles. The paint is thinned to a watery consistency. A good way to mix or thin the paint is to use film canisters. Use four to six drops of paint, then fill the canister about 1/3 full with water and mix. The line on the canister indicates how much water was used.

On the large areas to be painted, use a 1/4 inch flat brush.

Black was used for the hat and robe. The bottle was printed ivory black. Ivory is white, isn't it?

Maroon was thinned and used on the skirt. A 1/16 inch round brush was used to get in the tight spots.

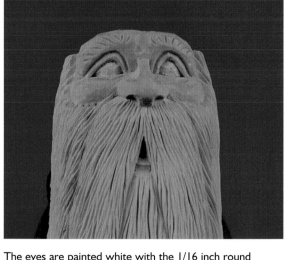

Basic white was used on the hair, beard, mustache, and crystal ball. Do not paint the eyebrows yet. Remove the hat for easier painting and paint the top of the head where the eyehole is located.

The eyes are painted white with the 1/16 inch round brush. A smaller brush may also be used.

Either add more black to the canister or make a new darker mix by adding more drops. When mixed, paint the collar.

Did you hear someone cough?

A medium flesh was applied to the face, lip, and hands.

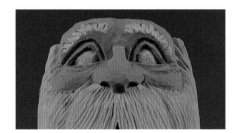

Now is the time to paint the white on the eyebrows.

The gold is really enhancing this piece.

Acrylic gold was used on the hat brim, cape border, robe border, and cuff border. The gold was not thinned as much. About 1/8 of the canister was filled with water. Also, paint under the hat where the cardboard was removed.

Draw in stars and quarter moons on the cuffs, robe border, and hat brim. Using the collar black, paint the stars and moons.

After painting all the stars and moons with black, overlay them with silver. This is a textured silver. Do not cover all the black with silver. Leave just a hint of black around the edges.

Navy blue was applied to the eye, forming the iris. After the blue has dried, place a white dot or highlight on each eye. I hear breathing!

Apply a light coat of burnt umber to the staff.

To highlight the face and hands, start by wetting these areas with clear water. Dip the brush in maroon paint then dry the brush so it will only leave a very small amount on the brush. Apply the dry brush maroon to the cheeks, lip, nose, and around the knuckles of the hands.

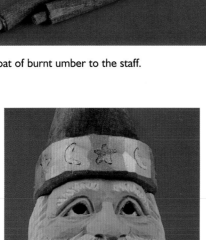

Using the darker black mixture, paint the pupil on the eyes.

Using the dry brush technique, apply navy blue to the crystal ball. This is a very light brushing.

Thin the textured silver to a watery consistency and apply to all of the robe and hat ... but not to the borders or collar.

It is hard to tell in this photo, but the carving has been sealed with two coats of clear matte spray.

Paint the lens cover, bottom of the carving, and inside the tapered area with the same gold paint used on the borders.

Three coats of additional clear finish have been applied to the crystal ball to give it a glossy look.

With a 1/2 inch brush, apply a coat of acrylic antiquing to small sections at a time. With a damp cloth, remove as much antiquing as desired. Do not apply the antiquing unless the carving has been sealed with the matte spray.

Antiquing has been applied and removed, leaving just enough.

Another view showing how the carving looks after antiquing.

Installing the Collide-A-Scope Components

Start by cleaning one of the two lenses. While holding the lens by the edge, apply two or three small drops of silicone glue to the surface. The glue should be as close to the edge as possible. Place the lens on a 1 inch dowel rod, glue side up.

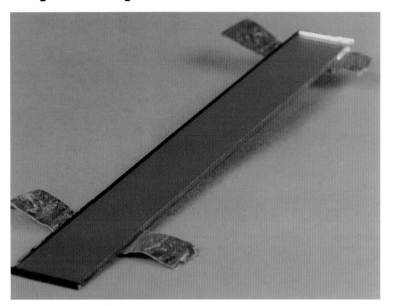

Remove the backing from the two short pieces of foil tape. Apply the tape to the back of one piece of mirror, 1 inch from the ends. Center the mirror on the tape.

While the dowel is being held either by hand or vise, place the carving over the lens. Lower the carving until it rests on the lens. Make sure the lens is at the eyehole. Look through the eyehole to see if there is any silicone glue visible. If so, remove lens, clean, then repeat the step. Place the carving upside down so the lens will not fall out while drying.

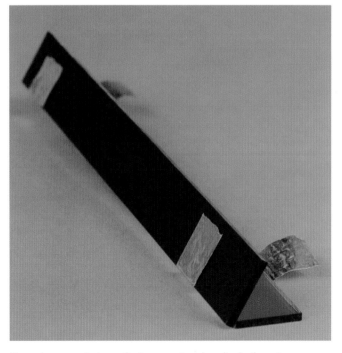

Place the second piece of mirror on its edge. Angle the mirror approximately 45 degrees as pictured. Apply the ends of the tape to the mirror back.

When the third piece of mirror is placed, it will complete an equilateral triangle. Apply the ends of the tape.

Remove the backing from one of the long pieces of foil tape and apply it to the edge of mirrors. Repeat this step two more times.

Open the mirrors up and thoroughly clean. Must be clean, clean!

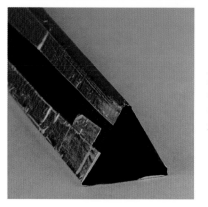

All edges should be taped and excess cut from the ends. Make sure there is no tape on the ends of the mirrors.

After the mirrors have been cleaned, fold them back into the equilateral triangle.

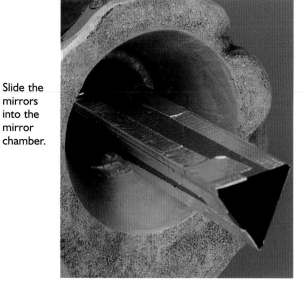

Slide the mirrors into the mirror chamber.

With a small dowel rod, push pieces of Styrofoam down the sides of the mirrors. This is done to hold the mirrors in place. Make sure the eyehole is in the center of the triangle. If not, the mirror can be adjusted by pushing one side of the Styrofoam tighter. This will move the mirrors.

Put a small amount of instant glue on one ring of the marble holder. Place the holder on the lens cover. Make sure the holder is centered over the opening. Let the glue dry.

Clean the remaining lens, then place it on the end of the mirrors.

Apply instant glue around the edge of the lens cover. Push the holder and cover into the opening until it rests against the lens. Let the glue dry.

While the holder and lens cover are drying, glue the staff in place. Also, glue the end of the staff to the robe. This is just a preventive measure. Most people hold the Collide-A-Scope in this area while viewing.

If the marble holder and lens cover have dried long enough, then snap that marble baby in place and start scoping! Turn the marble, not the carving.

Gallery

Uncle Sam

Uncle Sam is about 14 inches tall.

Instead of a marble in the base, Uncle Sam has a gem chamber. The carving must be turned to see all of the beautiful colors.

Uncle Sam

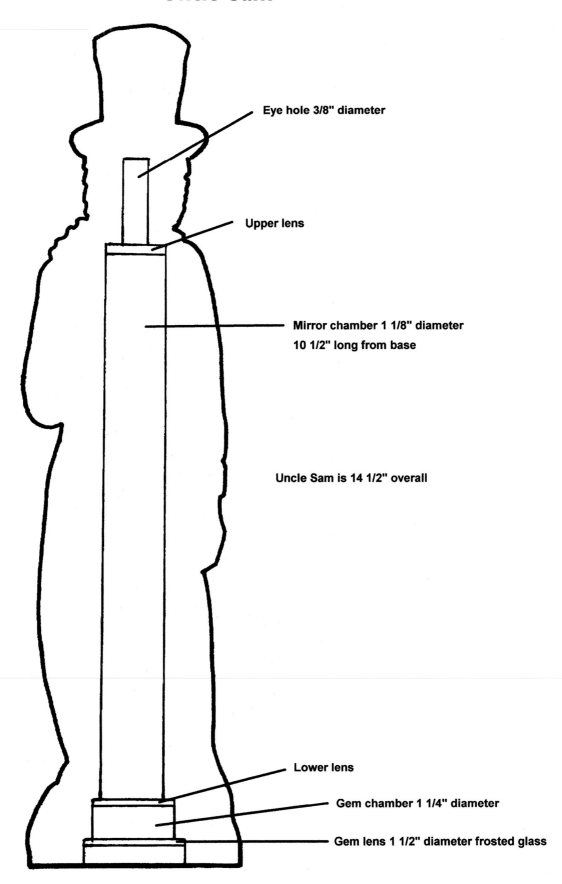

Eye hole 3/8" diameter

Upper lens

Mirror chamber 1 1/8" diameter
10 1/2" long from base

Uncle Sam is 14 1/2" overall

Lower lens

Gem chamber 1 1/4" diameter

Gem lens 1 1/2" diameter frosted glass

Fireman Santa

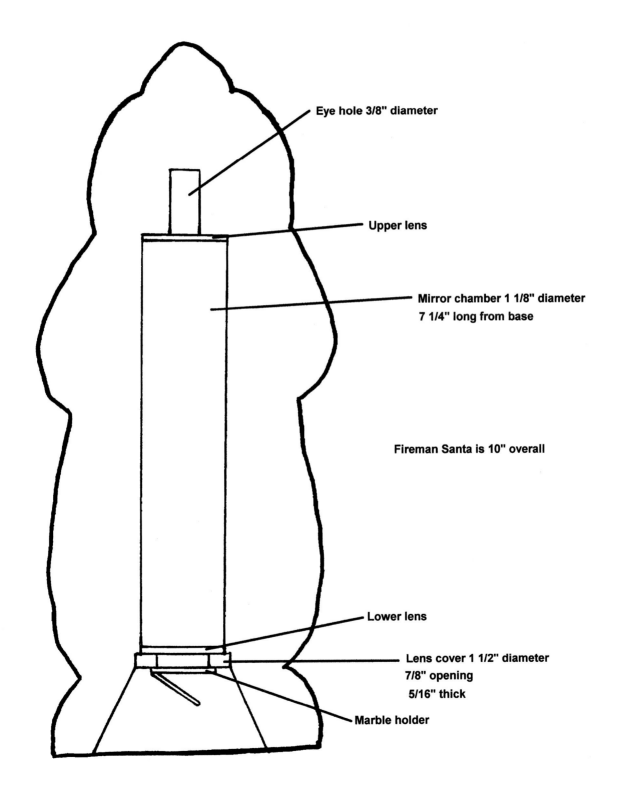

Eye hole 3/8" diameter

Upper lens

Mirror chamber 1 1/8" diameter
7 1/4" long from base

Fireman Santa is 10" overall

Lower lens

Lens cover 1 1/2" diameter
7/8" opening
5/16" thick

Marble holder

Fireman Santa

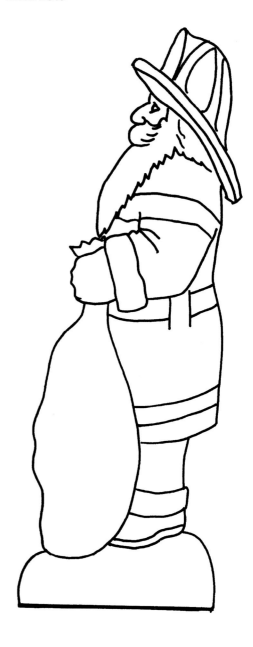

*Enlarge
133 1/3%
for original
size.*

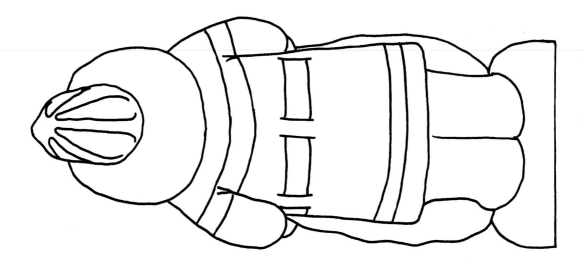

Old World Santa

Yes, that is right!. The tree must be removed to view those beautiful colors.

Old World Santa

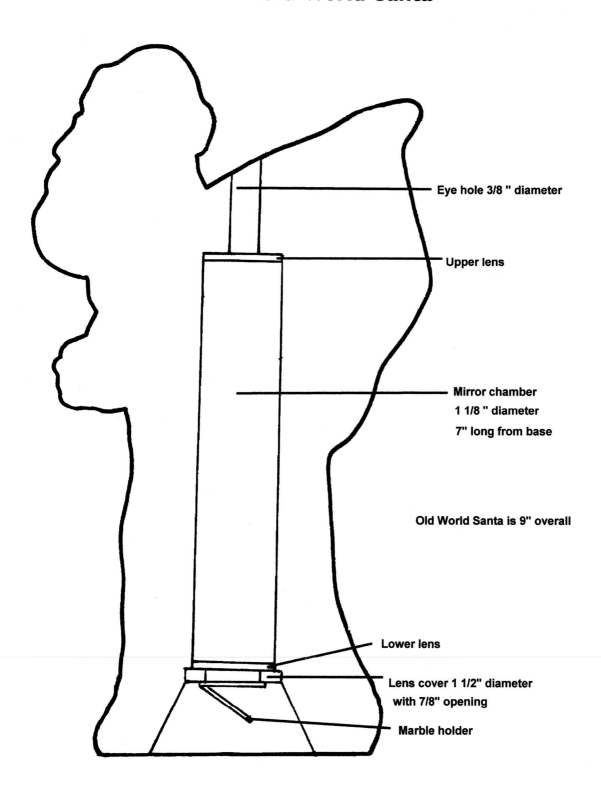

Eye hole 3/8 " diameter

Upper lens

Mirror chamber
1 1/8 " diameter
7" long from base

Old World Santa is 9" overall

Lower lens

Lens cover 1 1/2" diameter
with 7/8" opening

Marble holder

Enlarge
133 1/3%
for original
size.

Santa Rocket

Santa Rocket

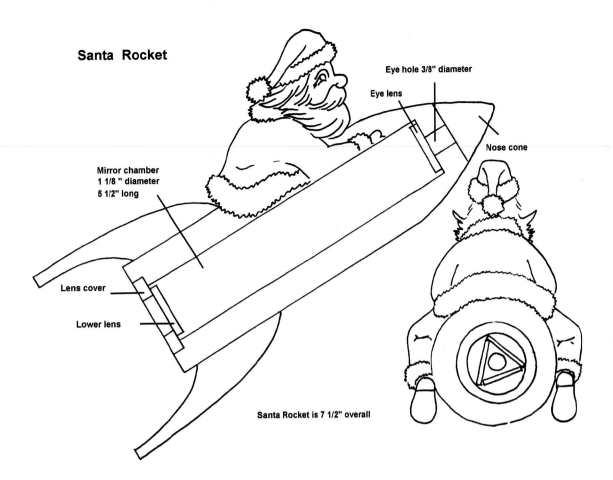

Eye hole 3/8" diameter

Eye lens

Nose cone

Mirror chamber
1 1/8 " diameter
5 1/2" long

Lens cover

Lower lens

Santa Rocket is 7 1/2" overall

*Enlarge 166 2/3 % for
original size.*

SANTA ROCKET

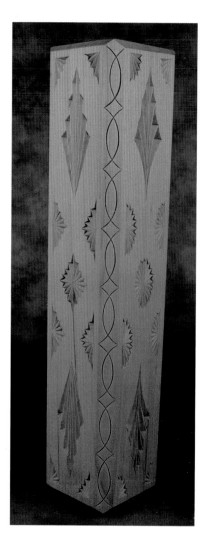

Chip Carving

All Collide-A-Scopes featured in the gallery are available in kit form. Check with your local carving supplier or the author.

This kit was carved by chip carving instructor, Darian Bebout, of Andover, Kansas.

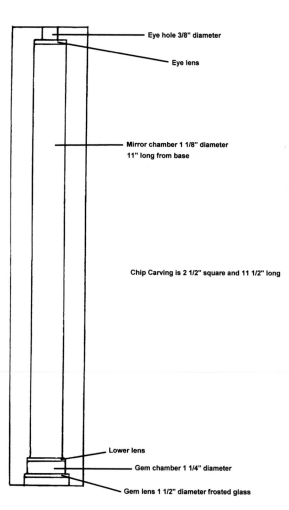

Eye hole 3/8" diameter

Eye lens

Mirror chamber 1 1/8" diameter 11" long from base

Chip Carving is 2 1/2" square and 11 1/2" long

Lower lens

Gem chamber 1 1/4" diameter

Gem lens 1 1/2" diameter frosted glass

Enlarge 166 2/3 % for original size.